Becoming a Beetle

by Grace Hansen

CHANGING ANIMALS

Abdo Kids Jumbo is an Imprint of Abdo Kids
abdopublishing.com

abdopublishing.com

Published by Abdo Kids, a division of ABDO, P.O. Box 398166, Minneapolis, Minnesota 55439.
Copyright © 2019 by Abdo Consulting Group, Inc. International copyrights reserved in all countries.
No part of this book may be reproduced in any form without written permission from the publisher.
Abdo Kids Jumbo™ is a trademark and logo of Abdo Kids.

052018

092018

 THIS BOOK CONTAINS
RECYCLED MATERIALS

Photo Credits: Alamy, iStock, Minden Pictures, Shutterstock, ©NHPA p.5/Photoshot

Production Contributors: Teddy Borth, Jennie Forsberg, Grace Hansen

Design Contributors: Dorothy Toth, Laura Mitchell

Library of Congress Control Number: 2017960557

Publisher's Cataloging-in-Publication Data

Names: Hansen, Grace, author.

Title: Becoming a beetle / by Grace Hansen.

Description: Minneapolis, Minnesota : Abdo Kids, 2019. | Series: Changing animals |
    Includes glossary, index and online resources (page 24).

Identifiers: ISBN 9781532108143 (lib.bdg.) | ISBN 9781532109126 (ebook) |
    ISBN 9781532109614 (Read-to-me ebook)

Subjects: LCSH: Beetles--Juvenile literature. | Animal life cycles--Juvenile literature. |
    Insects--Metamorphosis--Juvenile literature. | Animal behavior--Juvenile literature.

Classification: DDC 571.876--dc23

Table of Contents

Stage 1

All beetles begin as eggs.

Female beetles often lay

their eggs on leaves or wood.

4

Eggs are tiny and oval shaped. They are usually white or yellow in color.

Stage 2

A beetle hatches from its egg after a few days. But it does not look like an adult beetle. It is a beetle larva.

9

A **larva's** main job is to eat and grow. Different larva species eat different things. These include plants, soil, and rotting wood. Some even eat **manure**!

11

The **larva molts** as it grows. When it is big enough, it molts one last time.

Stage 3

This new skin makes a hard case around the larva.

This stage can last up to 9 months. Big changes happen during this time!

Stage 4

When the beetle is ready,
it splits the case open and
crawls out.

19

It is an adult beetle now! Adult beetles eat and find **mates**. Soon, female beetles will lay more eggs. And the cycle will begin again.

21

More Facts

- Beetles come in many sizes, colors, and shapes.

- There are more than 350,000 known kinds of beetles in the world.

- Beetle **larvae** can **molt** up to 15 times before they **pupate**.

22

Glossary

larva – the early form of an insect that at birth or hatching does not look like its parents and must grow and change to become an adult.

manure – an animal's solid waste.

mate – one of a pair of animals that will have young together.

molt – to shed skin that will be replaced by new skin.

pupate – become a pupa. A pupa is an insect in its inactive, immature form between larva and adult.

23

Index

Abdo Kids ONLINE
FREE! ONLINE MULTIMEDIA RESOURCES

Visit **abdokids.com** and use this code to access crafts, games, videos, and more!

Abdo Kids Code:
CBK8143